"*Ronnie Ann Ryan knows what she's talking about. At 40, she had a great job, good friends, and an enviable lifestyle, but she wanted one more thing: To meet The One and get married. Unfortunately, she hadn't dated in years and had zero prospects. With savvy, determination, and a sense of adventure, Ronnie turned her love life around, met The One, and married him. Now, more than 10 years later, she's still happily married to him. If you're ready for a lasting love that will truly make you happy, you owe it to yourself to take every word in Ronnie's book to heart.*"

—Terry MacDonald
DatingAdviceAlmostDaily.com

Why Can't I Find Love?

How to Transform Toxic Thoughts That Keep You From Love

Ronnie Ann Ryan, MBA, CCC

- The Dating Coach -

The Charmed Press, LLC
P.O. Box 417
Milford, CT 06460

All orders and inquiries should be addressed to:

Ronnie Ann Ryan
P.O. Box 417
Milford, CT 06460

Ronnie@nevertoolate.biz

Contents

Introduction...9
1. What's with the Shortage of Men?................. 11
2. Do You Believe "There's No Love for Me?" 15
3. Are You Prepared to Find Love?.....................17
4. Is It Too Embarrassing to Look for Love?.......21
5. Why Bother Looking for Love? 25
6. Get Off the Bitter Bus! 29
7. Tell Him to Stop Looking at Me!......................31
8. Does Your "Type" Limit Your Happiness?.......33
9. The Downside of Chemistry 37
10. What if I'm Bad at Picking Men?.....................41
11. But He Didn't Go to College............................45
12. Look Past the Paycheck to Find Love 49
13. Is the Alpha Male the Best Choice When
    Looking for Love?...53
14. Can You Help Me Get a Date with
    George Clooney? 57
15. The Problem with Mr. Twinkle Eye 61
16. I Want to Date a Man Just Like Me 65
17. Perfection Won't Keep You Warm at Night....69
18. Are You a "Yes" Person or a "No" Person?....73
19. Men are People Too 77
20. Give the Good Guys a Chance......................81
21. Open Your Heart to Love 85
22. Are Your Actions Aligned with Your
    Intentions and Desires?................................87
23. Self-Appreciation Increases Confidence
    for Dating..91
24. To Attract Love, Be Loving.............................93
25. Love is a State-of-Mind.................................97
26. Open to New Ways of Meeting Men............101
27. 9 Tips to Make Finding Love a Priority 105
28. Wrapping It All Up..109

Introduction

Working as a dating coach for over 10 years, I have encountered countless women who have what I call "toxic" beliefs they insist are true. Most don't even question the validity of these thoughts about single men, love and even themselves. Yet, these ideas are not only untrue; they are effectively keeping believers single and answer the question, "Why can't I find love?"

This book is a compilation of articles that address toxic thinking. You'll find help regarding your desire for instant chemistry, online dating, expectations about men, and building self-confidence.

I was devastated on my 40th birthday to realize I would probably be single for the rest of my life. Then, I turned everything around with the proven strategies I share today. I dated 30 men in 15 months to meet the adorable, supportive man who is now my husband. We've been happily married for more than 10 years and I thank my lucky stars every day. After the honeymoon, I decided my new mission was to help single women who are ready to take action, to find the love they want and deserve.

As you read through this book, see what resonates with you. Some chapters won't apply, but whatever you can shift to a more positive outlook will serve you well. In essence, it can open you up, making you emotionally available to meet the amazing man of your dreams. I found love over 40 which is why I know for sure, you can do it too.

Wishing you love,

Ronnie

- 1 -
What's with the Shortage of Men?

As a Dating Coach, clients ask me all sorts of questions. But one of the most frequent is a concern about seeing a shortage of men.

One client, Charlotte, told me that everywhere she's lived, people tell her there are no available men. For example, when she moved to Oregon at 32 for graduate school, local women felt there were no single men in town. Then she moved to Seattle two years later and was told it's a couples place and the locals aren't seen as friendly.

Later Charlotte moved to New York City where the problems of single women are legendary, followed by a move to Connecticut, a state filled with families and married folks. Next she moved to Spain to discover that her Spanish teacher and friends lament the shortage of men.

Charlotte wanted to know how to deal with hearing that there are no men wherever she is living and made it clear that she had no intention of moving to Alaska (all those men working on the oil pipeline). She also mentioned how curious it is that she has never once lived in a place where she felt, "Boy, am I lucky! This place is crawling with great, available guys!"

I hear you Charlotte, loud and clear! And I can see your frustration, but I don't agree with this feeling or believe there is a shortage. When you choose to work with me as your dating coach, I will challenge this type of belief that actually keeps you single. Think about other statements that people have made throughout history which were not true:

- ✧ Everyone said the earth was flat.
- ✧ Everyone said the Emperor's new clothes were fine.
- ✧ Everyone said sky lab would fall on our heads.
- ✧ Everyone said the computers would go wacky for Y2K.

Did any of these things happen? Were any of these things actually true? No, No, No!

In 1987, *Newsweek* ran an article that claimed a single woman 35+ had a better chance of getting abducted by terrorists than to get married. I think you know which one happened to me.

I suggest that Charlotte and all other single women ignore what people say. "They" (whoever they are) don't seem to have a very accurate track record with this type of generalized statement.

Instead, take a moment to remember a very important philosophical question: Is the glass half full or half empty? Truth be told, either way it's the same amount of liquid. The difference is based solely on your perspective. Whatever you focus on becomes your reality. I often quote this Universal principle from Hawaiian Shamanism: "Energy Flows Where Attention Goes."

The question is: Do you want your focus to be "There are no men"? I think not.

You will see that good men exist all around, and PS, you only need one right? The Universe is an amazingly abundant place so heighten your awareness of the abundant aspects by trying one of these exercises:
Count the leaves on any tree (or pine needles during the winter).

- ✧ Count the leaves.
- ✧ Count the stars in the night sky.
- ✧ Count the grains of sand on the beach.
- ✧ Count the blades of grass in your lawn or the park.

None of these things can really be counted and although each option does have an actual finite number — who can get there? That's the whole point. There are more available men than you can count, regardless of your location.

Here's the real challenge — how to start looking for evidence to prove there IS AN ABUNDANCE. This requires shifting your perspective and preventing yourself from falling back on old habits, seeing lack LACK.

Chances are very strong that you'll start to notice men that you never would have even seen before. That's because a person's mind will be open to collect new data using this perspective. And as Martha Stewart says, "That's a good thing."

I hope this perspective has opened your mind (and Charlotte's) and inspired you to start noticing the great men that are all around every day. One woman I know met her husband in WalMart —

she was walking in and she saw him walking out. Another met her husband in the dog park where they both walked their dogs and started talking. Still another met her long-term partner buying sheets in Bed, Bath, & Beyond. These bits of romantic kismet happen every day, everywhere. What will you do to make yourself available and cross paths with your soul mate?

Whether you choose to be of my over 40 dating coaching clients, I want to tell you to get out there, smile, be friendly, be grateful and aware of the great catch you are, and enjoy the wonderful life you have. This will make you highly attractive, get you out there, and help you cross paths with prospects to sort and find the right man. I did it, and that's why I know you can too.

- 2 -

Do You Believe
"There's No Love for Me?"

Do you tell yourself "There's No Love for Me"? This woe-is-me outlook on love is a syndrome that includes the following eight limiting beliefs:

- ✧ All the good men are taken.
- ✧ Love doesn't really exist or last.
- ✧ Who would want me? I'm too old, fat, unattractive, problematic, dull, baggage-ridden, etc.
- ✧ Men can't be trusted — they're all cheaters, liars, etc.
- ✧ I'll never find the right one for me.
- ✧ I'm too busy to date.
- ✧ I can't remember how to flirt or connect with men.
- ✧ Love is pain, that's why I want neither!

You've heard these beliefs or said them yourself because they are so prevalent today. As your dating coach, I think that's a sad statement. People today feel more and more isolated. So many of us work very hard, live at light speed cramming in too many responsibilities and taking little time for ourselves.

Working with me as your dating coach, you will quickly see how self-care and time out are crucial for a healthy, balanced life. And personal playtime or socializing is just as crucial. While you may feel you live a full and joyous solo life, if you long for love, you'll need to take steps to make it happen.

If you suffer from "There's No Love for Me" Syndrome and choose me as your dating coach, I'd assign you this surefire exercise to turn things around: Start seeing happy couples as you go about your day. Yes, they do exist! You might encounter them at the movies, at the grocery store, out to dinner, or walking down the street. Setting your internal radar on finding happy couples is one of the most powerful ways to re-wire your subconscious mind AND turn your dating karma around.

Countless people hold these limiting beliefs, so if these sound all too familiar, you are in no way alone! And sometimes just acknowledging this by itself can help to dissipate this negative outlook on love. In addition, when you start seeing happy couples, it refutes these negative thoughts, so you'll automatically have a much harder time hanging on to them and they will start to melt away.

I wouldn't do this dating coaching work if I didn't believe down to the core of my soul that finding love IS POSSIBLE! I turned these beliefs around for myself and found my husband. Every day another one of my clients makes this dramatic shift and her love life starts to blossom. Why not join the fun? See for yourself that love is available for you!

Are You Prepared to Find Love?

So many dating coaching clients ask me where the best places are to meet men. Surprisingly, this is often not the first step on the road to finding love. If you were to ask me, I would gingerly explain how it may seem that knowing the hot spots is the answer to your single circumstance, but is not the whole truth.

There is a step before meeting prospects that is actually vastly more important. The question becomes not where to meet the right men, but instead — WHO ARE YOU when you meet them?

In other words, what is your attitude and mind set when you look for love? Too frequently women go out with the scars of heartbreak and ex lovers written all over them. Perhaps you've had a run of bad dates or you haven't been out in years. If that's the case, there are three basic areas that might need strengthening to be the most attractive you can be.

1) Are You Emotionally Available?

As your dating coach, I want you to see that carrying a torch for a lost love, or remaining angry from love gone wrong drags your energy and attitude down. You cannot be your most alluring when carrying heavy-hearted baggage. Drop that baggage and free yourself up for a new relationship with these powerful exercises:

17

Light a candle and say a prayer. Ask for help from a higher power — such as a blessing and support for releasing your history. Ask to release what no longer serves you and sever any remaining emotional ties.

Visualize removing any imaginary strings of attachment that still connect you to a past love in your mind. Watch these strings dissolve or cut yourself loose. Then imagine healing the places on your body where the attachments occurred.

Take advantage of traditional therapy to facilitate the letting go process. Another approach is to work with an energy healer (Reiki, aroma-therapy, etc.) to release a past love.

2) Do You See Yourself as Someone Who Dates?

A woman who dates sees herself as attractive. She feels confident that men notice her and comfortable when they approach her. Her wardrobe includes alluring clothes that help her look and feel her best. So, as your dating coach, let me ask you, "What's in your closet and how would you respond if a man walked over to strike up a conversation?" If you've got a few date-worthy outfits and handle attention well, you're all set!

If you don't have anything appropriate to wear for a date, then you may avoid getting asked out. Interesting huh? When you sign up for dating coaching with me, you'll improve your self-image and hear how to handle male attention to feel confident in the singles scene.

3) Can You Flirt and Enjoy it for What it Is?

Flirting is an art that can be easily learned. When

you choose me as your dating coach, you'll hear that basic flirting includes brief eye contact followed by a smile before gracefully looking away. Using this simple tip can change your social karma dramatically. Clients who have tried this feel thrilled with the results! Why? Because it's so easy, it works and many women have forgotten the fundamentals of simply being friendly which is a very sad statement on life today.

Maybe it's all the bad news on TV or perhaps people are just too busy to bother being friendly. Whatever the reason, when you catch a man's eye, smile and act friendly, you let him know you are safe to approach. Believe it or not, most men don't like feeling rejected. They prefer a safe bet.

Most of all, the point of flirting is to have fun! When you smile at a man, you acknowledge him and that makes you both feel good. It's flattering and who doesn't enjoy a little flattery? Flirting works best without an agenda because then you feel relaxed and see this as fun. If you're trying to get someone's attention, your efforts aren't likely to seem natural.

AM I ?

If you're emotionally available, see yourself as an alluring person who dates, and know how to flirt, you're ready to attend singles events! Get out there to connect with the countless good guys who are waiting to meet a wonderful woman like you.

- 4 -

Is It Too Embarrassing
to Look for Love?

For many women, one of the biggest roadblocks to finding love is feeling too embarrassed to tell anyone you're looking. As your dating coach, I'll share the most frequent reasons women feel embarrassed about looking for love and I'll tell you new ways to see these concerns to dissipate your discomfort.

There must be something wrong with me because I'm still single

Women's liberation made it possible for women to support themselves, and the sexual revolution of the 1960's eliminated the stigma of intimacy before marriage. Both factors contributed to women's independence and at the same time, made it easier for men to avoid marriage. Today, many people put off tying the knot in favor of career. Plus, a divorce rate of nearly 50% has produced an abundance of singles who traditionally, would have stayed married.

The point is, if you're single, you don't need to feel alone. Nearly half of American adults are single.

It's not natural to look. Why can't I bump into him in my daily life?

Of course you might meet someone this way. But how long can you wait for serendipity to occur? When you were 22, almost everyone was available. At that age people are more social and spend a lot of time in group activities or bars, but neither holds as much appeal in mid-life.

As time marches forward, people feel more set in their ways, which is precisely why it's necessary to break from routine and do things you wouldn't normally do! Plus, over 30, there are a lot more people who are married so you are better off meeting qualified prospects — i.e., single men, the very point of attending singles events.

What will people think if they know I'm looking?
There are only three categories of people you might ask for help finding a blind date.

- ✧ A married person who already has a mate, so what negative opinion could be here?
- ✧ A single person who's in the same boat so what kind of judgment could she have?
- ✧ A divorced person who might make negative comments, but divorce can be painful so take the comments with a grain of salt.

Almost everyone is with a partner or wants to be. Romantic partnership is a natural human desire and nothing to be ashamed of.

I don't want to seem desperate
If you were looking for a job, wouldn't you tell everyone? The best way to find a job these days is through word of mouth. Nothing like a good referral and that is exactly what a blind date is - a referral! You might be surprised how excited people can get about matchmaking. Some even say they get points in heaven! So why not give people a chance to earn a few points?

On the other hand, how you ask influences people more than the question itself. Word choice and tone of voice are key. Tell people in an upbeat manner that you'd like to meet someone. Try, "Life is good and I'd like to share it with someone." You'll see there is nothing desperate about wanting to share.

As you can tell, these worries are mostly unfounded and simply not true. Asking people if they know anyone for you may feel awkward at first, but nothing that a little practice can't cure!

My Success Story
When I was single and serious about finding love, I told everyone I knew and everyone I met, that I was looking for the right man. One night I was talking to a woman I'd just met about wanting to meet Mr. Right. Before I could ask, she simply volunteered to help by insisting that I meet her brother. I gave her my number, her brother called, we met and he's now my husband! Think about what would have happened if I'd been too shy to say anything?

Whether or not you decide to work with me, I'd suggest not to ignore one of the most powerful methods to generate love-life prospects. The cost of not asking is very high. For myself, I might still be looking.

Enlist the help of your network of friends, family, acquaintances and a dating coach like me. Start slowly with the people who feel the safest. With practice, you're sure to feel braver. The sooner you try it, the sooner you can reap the benefits — finding the love you desire!

- 5 -
Why Bother Looking for Love?

"Dear Dating Coach,

I'm 52 years old and have been divorced for over 10 years. I've tried so many of the options you have suggested to meet men without any success. Honestly I feel like I'm at that point where this question keeps coming to mind, why bother? It feels so much easier to just enjoy my life as it is, even though I'd really like a companion. What are your thoughts?

Bothered in Wilton"

Dear Bothered,
It's understandable that having tried and not found what you want, you feel frustrated. However, what really stands out for me is a portion of your last statement — "It's easier to enjoy my life as it is." This feeling is filled with wisdom. Regardless of where you are in life, especially when it comes to desires/goals, it's always smart to enjoy what you do have and what is going well.

Upbeat Perspective
I learned this upbeat perspective while getting my coaching certification — one instructor insisted that clients begin sessions by appreciating the good things that are already part of life. (Complaining feels so much easier for everyone!) Shifting to a grateful perspective will lift your spirits dramatically if you stick with it for just a full minute or two. It's really quite surprising what a powerful exercise this is.

Expand Your World

It's crucial to understand why you want a partner. If you are looking for a mate to expand your world, it is better to expand it yourself first. Take an adult education class. Learn a new skill or hobby. Join a gym or take yoga. Play bridge with a group. Do volunteer work. Any of these activities opens up new doors by stimulating your mind, meeting new people, enriching your life, and adding to the fun.

Powerful Phenomenon

When you are happy with what you have, that potent message is broadcast out into the Universe, making you far more attractive than when you bemoan what you don't have. It's a very curious and dynamic phenomenon. So, go ahead and enjoy your life as it is. And, at the same time you can still want more, expand your options, and look for the company of a loving partner who will add even more joy to your life. It's a subtle distinction that can make a world of difference.

Icing on the Cake

The next time you feel ready to get back out there and resume your search, go with this new attitude — Life is good and a partner to share it with is the icing on the cake. Now you aren't lonely or sad, you are a whole, healthy, confident, attractive person looking for a mate to share life with.

Positive Facts about Dating

Please keep these positive dating facts in mind:

- ✧ There are 42 million singles in the United States over the age of 40.
- ✧ Since the year 2000, the number of people on Match.com over the age of 50 has tripled!

- ✧ Over 12% of marriages and 20% of relationships started online.

- ✧ According to a survey on relationships conducted by AARP, 75% of singles between the ages of 40 - 70 plan on finding a new romantic partner to share life with.

- ✧ There are many dating sites that focus on the 50+ crowd. Just Google "Dating over 50," you'll find all kinds of options to try.

So, when you're ready to work with me as your dating coach and get back out there, keep this thought in mind "It's never too late to find the love you want." People find love everyday and if you're active, you could be next!

- 6 -
Get Off the Bitter Bus!

Are you on the Bitter Bus? What? You never heard of that before? Well it sure is a descriptive euphemism for feeling down on dating.

When you feel negative about the singles' scene, you actually sabotage your prospects. Feeling happy, positive and open, are much better emotions. Before you choose me as your dating coach, let me tell you a few tips to get you off the bitter bus and on to a more positive dating experience:

When you catch yourself saying negative things about dating and men, wake up! Stop yourself at the moment you realize the bus is rolling and you are on it. Change the subject you are talking about or move on to happier thoughts.

Don't put down the attempts your friends or family make to meet new people. Be supportive instead because you'd like to see them happy wouldn't you? When you are positive for others, you will be more positive for yourself — it's a good habit to adopt.

Don't assume because you tried a particular singles' event or meeting method one time, that you'll have the same poor results if you try again. It could happen, but you could also meet someone, so give yourself a chance.

Someone else's good luck at finding a mate is evidence that it's still possible for you to find love

29

too! Instead of feeling like other people are luckier than you are, why not think "If that person can find someone, so can I!"

Generalities hurt you. Not all men are liars, cheats, commitment-phobes, etc. There are always exceptions to every rule and who says this poor behavior is a rule? Everyone is not the same thankfully or we'd all like the same man. Yikes, what a horrible thought that is!

Stop riding the Bitter Bus. As your dating coach, I ask you to try any of these steps to shift your attitude and improve your chances of finding the love you want. When you choose to work with me, I'll help you turn these blocks around for greater dating success.

- 7 -

Tell Him to Stop Looking at Me!

One of my Dating Coaching clients complained about men who look at her. These are men she isn't thrilled with and men she wouldn't choose to date. She wanted to know how to get them to stop looking at her "like that."

I explained that if she really thinks about it — she wants them to look. The last thing you want is for men not to look at you. When men check you out, they acknowledge your attractiveness, your allure, your beauty. Otherwise they wouldn't be looking.

Now I realize you might not like all the guys who look at you, or the way they look at you. But so what? Honestly, what can you do about that? Be angry and tell the guy to "buzz off?" That's not productive or a good use of your energy because it will not make you appear more attractive.

Instead — why not appreciate the fact that these men are appreciating you? It's the truth. You don't have to talk to them, date them or marry them. But, you can be thankful for the evidence of your attractiveness that they have shared with you.

OK, this may sound silly. But one thing I can tell you for sure is that when you are thankful (internally, not verbally) you send out a message of thanks to the Universe. And that is very attractive and highly magnetic. Think of Sarah Ban Breathnach's book, *Simple Abundance* — she's all about being grateful.

Well guess what — the grateful attitude works here too. And whether or not you choose to work with me, I have many happy clients who agree that being grateful for male attention works.

So the next time a man looks you up and down and you get angry or creeped out, think again. Remember this is evidence of your feminine allure so let it build your confidence. Say "Thank you" in your mind and walk away feeling good about yourself. When you sign up for dating coaching with me, this is the kind of thing you'll start to feel better about. After all, some guy would be darn lucky to be dating a great woman like you.

- 8 -

Does Your "Type" Limit Your Happiness?

Do you have a type? You know what I mean. Do the people you date have similarities, in the way they look, lifestyle, or personality characteristics? Your type may be a tall guy with blonde hair and blue eyes. You may be attracted to older, distinguished or accomplished men. Perhaps you like excitement and drama or have a penchant for saving lovers with lots of problems. Some are drawn to the more aloof person who is hard to get. These examples are all "types" of men.

So, what's wrong with having a "type?" Well nothing at all if it's working for you. If you are happy in your current relationship, feel the balance of power is acceptable, and the situation enjoyable — good for you! Unfortunately, having a type frequently presents the same relationship issues over and over again — a situation that is not always fun.

Many of my dating coaching clients complain they just don't meet men who are attractive. This is a tip off telling me you are hindering the dating search by seeking a specific "type" of man. Another signal is when someone says, "I just don't meet anyone interesting." It's a big world out there — there must be prospects who can spark your interest. If these comments sound familiar, you may be limiting yourself by "typecasting".

In case you've been wondering why your relationships often end with the same problems or you can't seem to meet anyone who does it for you, it's time to examine what each of your past partners had in common. What should you look for to discover a pattern? As your dating coach, I recommend considering the following aspects of your past lovers:

- ✧ Personality *good*
- ✧ Lifestyle choices ~ *OK*
- ✧ Family patterns and upbringing *✓*
- ✧ Outlook on life and attitude *positive*
- ✧ Physical characteristics ~ *NICE*
- ✧ Style of pursuing or dating you ~ *good*
- ✧ Communication patterns *good*
- ✧ Partying and addictions *NONE*
- ✧ Capability for intimacy *were great safe Bill*
- ✧ Flashiness vs. substance *—*
- ✧ Expectations and demands *to finish w/ much*
- ✧ Amount of time he spends with you, etc. *great*

Spend time getting to know who you are in a relationship and become familiar with your own patterns and expectations. This offers important clues for the next time you get involved or for your current circumstances.

Okay, you've looked at your patterns. Now, what do you do with that information? Keep in mind that knowledge helps you make better, more educated decisions. This is where the head meets the heart and the rubber meets the road in terms of dating effectiveness. After all, the purpose of dating is usually "data gathering" to find a good match for a long-term relationship or marriage. Awareness is the first step towards creating change.

Ask yourself, "Have these similarities in my choice of partners been good for me and produced the romantic relationship I want?" "Does this type of person meet my needs and make me happy?"

If you say, "not really," to these questions, you now have an opportunity to break from your traditional habits. The definition of insanity is doing the same thing over and over again, yet expecting a different result. Since that's not too productive, I recommend trying something new.

The next time you are "out there" looking for love, be open to new types of people who might be attractive and get along with you better. Perhaps you'll consider a more soft spoken and shy man who has a good heart versus the flashy, good-looking guy who is skilled at telling you what you want to hear. Or maybe you'll pick a more open and available man who doesn't play games and offers a genuine heart connection.

Push yourself beyond your usual attractions to explore a broader range of potential mates. Cast a wider net to let more lovable options flow into your world who may be better at satisfying your relationship needs. Leave your type in the dust and find a good match who will expand your world and create a more joyful, lasting partnership.

With 101 million single American adults, there is no doubt in my mind that the right person for you is out there. Choosing to work with me as your dating coach, we'll address the type of guy you seek so you can get a handle on how you might be limiting yourself.

The Downside of Chemistry

When I talk to my dating coaching clients, or ask women in general what qualities they seek in a man, inevitably the conversation turns to chemistry. Women say they know immediately whether there is that magical spark or not. But what is chemistry?

Here's what I get as a response:

handwritten notes in margin: part clearly, connection, emotional, feeling

✧ Chemistry is ha cha cha, spoken in a breathy voice.
✧ It's sparks and electricity.
✧ It's excitement and desire.
✧ It's an attraction that sizzles.
✧ It makes you melt.
✧ It's the stuff that sells romance novels.

So, what do all these descriptions have in common? Sex. Yup, that's what instant chemistry is really about. It's an intense sexual attraction that pulls two people together for an experience beyond the rational, thinking mind. Some women say without it, there isn't "real" love. At least that's what the media would have you believe.

Chemistry is exciting, magical, fast paced, and cannot be denied. Or can it? Let's look at both sides of chemistry to understand the advantages and drawbacks. After all, if so many women feel chemistry should dictate their relationship choices, it might be helpful to examine what's behind this mysterious driving force.

Advantage #1

With chemistry, you can count on a passionate sex life that rivals any Danielle Steele novel. Whether it's steamy, sweet, or tender, it will feel fantastic, highly memorable, and leave you breathless, wanting more.

Advantage #2

Chemistry is exciting and you feel incredibly alive with an electric-like passion. Often, the chemistry relationship falls into one of two camps: 1) Contact is limited because he's married, lives far away, you met him on vacation, etc., or 2) The relationship is established with lightening speed. Either way, the pairing is dramatic.

Advantage #3

Chemistry is richly romantic and feels like love; the swept off your feet variety. Every woman dreams of finding a romantic partner who appears magically like a knight in shining armor riding a white horse.

OK — go get a glass of cold water if you need one before moving on to the drawbacks.

Drawback #1

Chemistry often overwhelms and clouds a person's better judgment. The magnetic attraction can be compared to the classic story of the moth drawn to the flame. And what happens to the moth when it gets too close? The moth gets burned!

Many women admit they found chemistry with men who are "bad boys." These men can be romance junkies who love the chase, but disappear when the discussions start. Bad boys are terribly fun, but emotionally unavailable and even commitment phobic. They seem exciting, but not usually looking for long-term relationships.

When you know a man is bad for you, regardless of how right it feels when you're together, you are probably the victim of bad-boy chemistry. One clear sign is if you hear yourself saying "I just can't help it."

Drawback #2
People often mistake chemistry for love. But jumping into great sex may result in intimacy that's limited. So many times there just isn't any foundation beyond sizzling attraction and when that fades — there's not much left to work with. Solid long-term relationships are built on getting to know each other through a variety of shared experiences. That takes time and a partner with similar values and goals, who is willing to work through the inevitable relationship bumps.

Drawback #3
I'm all for romance, but the feeling that prince charming will suddenly ride into your life and sweep you off your feet is unlikely. Through talking to thousands of women it's become obvious that wildly romantic men are often in love with falling in love and don't often progress beyond the first stages of dating.

Set your sites on a man who can go the distance rather than someone who lavishes you with wine, roses, and empty sweet talk. You'll feel a lot happier in the long run and save yourself the heartache of trying to understand why the guy said so many wonderful things and then suddenly disappeared.

Overall, most women reluctantly admit that focusing on chemistry as the sole factor for selecting a man hasn't served them well. This choice leads them astray into relationships that have broken their hearts and been highly disappointing.

Don't get me wrong. When you work with me as your dating coach, I understand that attraction feels very important to any budding romance. The discussion is about insisting on chemistry as the benchmark for selecting the right man. Instead of relying on sexual attraction that harkens back to prehistoric times to ensure the survival of the species, think about all the qualities that will make for a loving, healthy partnership.

If you meet a nice guy who appears to have many of the qualities you desire, but falls a bit short on chemistry, cut him some slack. Get to know him better so you can appreciate who he really is and discover the kind of attraction that builds with time. For a loving partnership, kiss instant chemistry goodbye, and instead assess prospects based on qualities that have more meaning for the long haul.

There has to be
some sort of attraction.

- 10 -
What if I'm Bad at Picking Men?

Recently, I was speaking to old college friends about what else — dating! One friend, Allison, complained how the biggest obstacle to getting back out there to find a man is the fact that she hasn't chosen well in the past. "I have a history of picking the wrong men!" complained Allison.

As your dating coach, let me ask you — do you ever feel like this?

Do You Ignore What Men Say?
We talked about why Allison's previous beaus were not right for her. For the most part, she heard what the men said about themselves which should have disqualified them as partners. But she managed to ignore the red flags. For example, she spent eight years with one man who told her on the day they met that he never wanted to marry or have children. Children were a big goal for Allison.

But Allison was lonely and VERY attracted to him. She overlooked his comments and launched into the relationship. She thought his desires would change. Maybe she was only thinking for the moment. Now at 45, she looks back at this string of men and wishes she had listened to what they said to her.

Fear of Making the Wrong Choice Holds You Back
Allison bemoaned the fact she wasted time with these men and wished she had heeded the

warnings, had been smarter, had picked better. And looking forward, that is exactly what keeps her from trying again. "With such a bad history, why do I want more of the same?"

This sounds like an excellent question. However, it makes sense that no one wants to feel more of THE SAME. No. Who would go for more disappointment? When you choose to work with me as your dating coach, I can help you see at least three ways to avoid repeating your "bad picking" history:

1) Make a List of Things You Don't Want in a Man
I suggested something revolutionary to Allison. What if she made a list of the red flags that she had ignored in the past? Would that feel helpful? She laughed and asked sarcastically, "What would I do with the list? Stick it on the refrigerator?" I responded with a resounding "Yes!"

Make a short list of the 5 - 10 things you never want to see again in a relationship. Then copy the list and put one on the refrigerator, the bathroom mirror, in your purse, at your desk and maybe even on your night stand. For people who have ignored red flags and harbor regrets, this reminder is imperative and enormously helpful.

2) Learn from Past Mistakes
Second, remember that your past has made you who you are today. It formed you, shaped you and made you the rich character and personality that defines you. Your relationships are part of your life experience which hopefully made you smarter and wiser. It certainly can be true if you chose to look at things this way. As your dating coach, I strongly

advise it. Regret won't help you feel ready to move forward, but let me tell you, learning from your mistakes will.

3) The Past Does Not Dictate the Future
That's a true statement on all levels of life, from your love life to world politics. We cannot let the past dictate our future. But we can LEARN FROM IT! If you still want a loving relationship with a great man, please make your list of red flags and then get back out there to find the love you want and deserve. When a flag starts waving — PAY ATTENTION and notice if it's time to move on.

Do Not want a relationship
or Does not have time
= Not w you

Do not let him put you
into bed — work on
the emotional connection
NO Kissing
Learn from Regrets

- 11 -
But He Didn't Go to College

After about nine months of working with me as her dating coach and dating men, my client Dana found a keeper. She and Rex got along well and enjoyed each other's company. He called her often and they saw a lot of each other during the seven weeks of dating.

But Dana felt bothered by Rex's lack of education. He's a plumber and she has a master's degree. Dana wanted a man with a good education and felt confused. She said she was glad to meet such a great guy but what was my take on her education requirement?

I explained to Dana that a college degree won't keep her warm at night. While she has every right to want an educated man, bending the requirements can open doors and be a smart way to go.

Why? Not because she should "settle." I despise that word! Yet, loosening up on requirements allows a woman to meet more men which widens the pool of applicants. And that improves the chances for finding the right man. This applies to education, divorce, height, hair, income, or any number of criteria you have for screening potential suitors.

Regarding education specifically, my question to Dana was what will his college diploma do for her?

1) Some say that college is a right of passage and an accomplishment.
OK, I can see that, but there are certainly other measures of accomplishment beyond book learning and frat parties.

2) A man without college might not have much in common with her.
That doesn't seem to be the case here. You can still share interests and similar values regardless of education.

3) Attending college is a sign of intelligence.
I beg to differ on that one and have met many people with advanced degrees who don't possess a bit of common sense, social skills, or intelligence.

Oh yeah!

4) She wants to be sure she's on par intellectually.
But a college educated man could still be less equipped! College doesn't guarantee intelligence.

yup

I married a man without a college degree and it's working out fine even though I have an MBA. Over the years, he's learned more about marketing and business and I've learned quite a bit about mechanics and how things work. When I'm in need of a proofreader, he's my man. My MBA hasn't helped me with typos.

In addition, Paul reads the paper to keep up on current events, where I avoid the news because of its negativity. (Paul shares the highlights with me.) That's just another reason why we are a great pair! We COMPLIMENT EACH OTHER. We are not the same, but we fit together well.

As long as Dana feels she can have a good conversation and he gets who she is and what she is talking about - isn't that what counts? If Dana can find a way to relinquish this education requirement, she may discover she's found a wonderful life partner.

Whether or not you choose to work with me as your dating coach, I'll say, "Lighten up on requirements when-ever you can. The reward may just be the man of your dreams."

By the way, Dana recently wrote me a heart-felt thank you note. She and Rex just celebrated six months and are very happy. Dana thanked me for encouraging her to give Rex a chance and see if she could get past the education thing. She did and feels it was worth it! Wouldn't you like to write a note like this? Now, that is a note I'd love to read!

- 12 -
Look Past the Paycheck
to Find Love

Are you a successful career woman who would like to find a loving relationship? Have you felt frustrated by the men you meet and feel they are not your equal? You may be wondering if you'll ever meet a man who measures up and you are not alone in this plight.

As women have taken on more traditionally male high-powered jobs, this has created a strong ripple effect on their love lives. In times past, women often married up, using their good looks or background to get a man who was considered a "good provider." But, if women are going to occupy many of those "good provider" jobs, perhaps they can loosen up the need for Mr. Equal Income and think of other important qualities that a life partner can offer.

For example, this study conducted by Michael R. Cunningham, a psychologist and professor of communication at the University of Louisville demonstrates a shift in priorities that has already occurred. He asked college women if, upon graduation, they would prefer to marry a high school teacher who works short days, has summers off and energy to help raise children, or a top-earning surgeon who works a heavy schedule. Three-quarters of the women chose the teacher!

Here are some ground-breaking facts paraphrased from a 9/23/07 New York Times article entitled

"Putting Money on the Table" by Alex Williams. For the first time in history, 20 something women who work full time in big American cities like New York, Chicago, Boston and Minneapolis, are earning more than the same age men, based on an analysis of 2005 census data by Andrew Beveridge, a Queens College sociology professor.

This gap stems from a significant difference in education — 53 percent of women in their 20s, working full time, are college graduates, compared to 38 percent for men. Plus, more women have graduate degrees.

Ouch — that gap is definitely going to require rethinking marriage partner potential isn't it? And that shift is happening for women in their 20s as noted above. But this change is happening at many levels.

I have several college friends who were earning over $200,000 in high powered jobs who married men that were not their professional equals. One friend married the manager of a small inn where she stayed on vacation in the south of France and another married a man who was the personal assistant to a wealthy business man. They are happy couples with children and it's working out very well for them.

Personally I married a man who didn't graduate from college. Even though I have an MBA, I figured his education didn't have to be a factor in my MRS. He's kind, adorable, generous, emotionally available, and supportive. He can pretty much fix anything, leaves his job at work and comes home to make me tea in the afternoon. I don't think I'm lacking for much as a result of his not being my education or career equal.

You can say I settled if you want. And I'll even agree — I settled for a heart of gold and a happy relationship with a really good man.

If you are a highly successful woman reading this, and you'd like to find love, maybe it's time to think about working with me as your dating coach and the qualities that would work for you in a romantic partner. You want him to be employed and financially independent? That's fair. But how much money he makes might not be the most important criteria for relationship success. It's time to look past the paycheck to find the love you want and deserve.

- 13 -

Is the Alpha Male the Best Choice When Looking for Love?

One of my clients, Nancy, wrote to thank me for my coaching and encouragement with her dating life. While her journey has taken many twists and turns, she feels I have helped her open new doors and possibilities for love.

Nancy is a hard-driving professional woman in her late 40s. Traditionally, her taste in men has been what she describes as the "Alpha Male," a take-charge kind of guy who is a hard-driving businessman. Usually, this type of guy is very exciting, unpredictable and lacking in emotional capacity. The relationships have left her angry and hurt. But she's always felt attracted to men like this — until recently.

Through coaching, Nancy started to consider what other qualities might work for her in a partner. Maybe a man who has some emotional intelligence, who can talk about his feelings, be true to her and sensitive to her needs as well. Someone who can be supportive as well as decisive and confident.

The big news is that Nancy became much more aware of how she feels about men. She was shocked by her own internal chatter which is not positive and she realized she didn't really like men. Nancy suddenly had insight into the fact that she often talked to men like they were idiots. She realized these are not the thoughts of an alluring woman on the lookout for a loving partnership!

Following my dating coaching advice, Nancy started to talk to men like regular people and feel respect for them. She allowed herself to become interested in almost any man who approached her — not that she had to date every guy, but simply talk to him for the simple pleasure of discovering who that person is. And guess what Nancy discovered? All men are not disappointing, rotten, untrustworthy, arrogant jerks. Turns out some are very interesting and worth talking to. And a few are really wonderful.

The good news? Nancy met Don at a singles' gathering. Even though he drove a Porsche which made him look like her usual type, he definitely was not. Don is sensitive, eager, and lacks that "alpha" personality that she used to feel lured in by. But she kept thinking, "Hey, give this guy a chance. He sounds like a nice person and might be interesting."

Nancy and Don have been out on six dates and are taking things slowly. She has moments where she questions what she's was doing since he's just not her type. Yet, Nancy has enjoyed his company and Don keeps asking her out. The slower pace also feels good because she's taking the time to really get to know him. Interestingly enough, the more she finds out, the more she likes him.

While the jury is still out on the long-term potential for Nancy and Don, she feels that Don is a gem. He's considerate, thoughtful, sweet, communicative, and fun. Nancy finds herself in totally new territory and that adds to the excitement she feels.

This is a perfect example of how crucial opening up to new types of men can be, to be aware of and shift your inner thoughts and attitude towards men, and take the time to give someone a chance. So far, so good!

Whenever a dating coaching client tells me she is dating someone totally different, I feel very excited. That's because, when you break away from your usual type, you have a chance to see someone who could be a better match. People often stay trapped in thinking a specific type is the only kind of person who can make them happy. Not true! In fact, someone's type is more often the kind of person who will deliver the same heartbreak that makes you want to stop dating entirely.

Get out there and discover new personalities that will feel right to you and offer you the relationship you have been dreaming about. People fall in love every day. Relax some of your rigid requirements, then open your mind and heart to let a great man in.

I don't have a usual type just needs to be financially ok

Can You Help Me Get a Date with George Clooney?

One of my dearest dating coaching clients sent me numerous emails with this request — Can you get me a date with George Clooney? I hate to say no, but what's my choice really? I don't know the guy. I know WHO HE IS, but I don't KNOW him.

But what about Six Degrees to Kevin Bacon — that game which claims you are just six people away from anyone you want to meet, if you utilize your network well. We all know approximately 250 people, so if you do the math, you can get connected to Kevin, or George in this case, with just six connections.

Where am I going with this? A very wealthy woman, Olivia, took one of my dating classes recently. In her 60's and still stunning, she wore a St. John's suit, her hair was perfectly coiffed, and she was decked out with great accent jewelry. (I always notice the jewels.) Totally put together. Very Jackie O.

After class she approached me, waiting until everyone else had left to ask me how she could meet eligible men her age with "means" who were healthy, active, and not looking for a "nurse and a purse." That made me laugh because I had never heard that expression — obviously I don't travel in the "right circles." Not that age bracket, not that bank account either — Boca Raton and the Hamptons.

Now let's think about this — Olivia is asking ME where the men of means are — but she's the one traveling in "those" circles. Or, maybe not. What's amiss here is that she's not out there being social any more. As people get older, sometimes their social circles get smaller. Olivia admitted this was sadly true.

To combat the natural social attrition from your life, you have to reach out and meet new people. I told her to play bridge, volunteer where other wealthy women do (museums, art galleries, politics?) and meet new girlfriends if nothing else. Go to polo matches, boat shows, or golf tournaments. Online, you might meet a wealthy man just as easy as a poor one on Match.com or MatureSingles.com.

Here's what I tell my dating coaching clients. Rich or poor, the search process is pretty much the same. A friend of mine went to a socialite wedding of two wealthy people who met on — you got it — Match. com. Yes, it really happened!

So if you are looking for a person of means, you'll have to start traveling in those circles. Go to expensive restaurants and sit alone at the bar on a Thursday night. Volunteer for socialite causes. Participate in political fund raisers. Go where the upwardly mobile folks go and hang out. Meet their friends. Expand your world. That's true for whatever type of person you want in any income bracket. The socializing price tag and addresses may be different, but the process is always the same. Who knows — you just might meet George Clooney or somebody better!

- 15 -

The Problem with
Mr. Twinkle Eye

One of my over 40 dating coaching clients was explaining the type of guy she is looking for. Suzanne, who is 51, successful, bright, energetic and friendly, seeks a man with some passion and that certain something she can only describe as "a twinkle in his eye."

As a dating coach, I hear things like this all the time. Certain descriptors look like neon flashing lights to me because I've heard them so many times. As a result, I've caught on to a few things and "twinkle" definitely has a specific meaning.

I asked Suzanne how she feels about George Clooney. Does George have the twinkle she's seeking? Suzanne replied "Oh yes — he's got it!"

Just today, my dating coaching client Bethany told me about a new guy she had a date with. "He's just my type, edgy, successful, and has a twinkle in his eye." I'm not kidding. This twinkle thing shows up all over the place, virulent, and spreading like the blight that killed elm trees years ago. However, this blight is infecting over 40 daters, keeping many women unhappily single.

Bethany agreed with the George Clooney example. She went on to tell me the "twinkling" details that draw her in over and over again. "Mark has energy, passion about his work, a brilliant mind and is so charming. Yet, he is aloof, emotionally unavailable, and hasn't called me for a second date yet. I'm tired of men who behave this way."

I shocked Bethany with my next comment. "Did you know that a charming man with a twinkle in his eye will almost always be a package deal with the qualities you don't like such as aloof and emotionally unavailable?" Bethany started thinking back on all the twinkling eyes she met and felt totally shocked. She couldn't believe she had never put those two things together before.

If you are holding out for the George Clooney type, beware of what you really seek — a bad boy who is most likely unattainable. For whatever reason, people often want what they can't have — it's that much more desirable and simply human nature.

I told both of my dating coaching clients that they might consider other qualities in a man. What else would make them happy? What other personality traits would sound attractive? I asked them to give this some serious thought because for them, a healthy love life depends on this discovery.

In addition, I pointed out that if they wanted to avoid wasting time with the wrong man, they need to notice if a guy is "twinklicious" much more quickly. If the answer is "yes", these women better pay attention to the red flags they hear. Get very clear that Mr. Twinkle Eye is not Mr. Right.

When you sign up for dating coaching with me, you'll feel supported and gain these powerful insights into your own dating behavior. If you insist on a certain type of guy, twinkle or not, I highly recommend expanding your idea of what type of man suits you if you want to find lasting love.

When a dating coaching client calls me and says," I'm dating this guy who is so different than most of the men I've dated." I know something wonderful is about to happen! It's a sure thing almost every time I get that call — that woman has found lasting love.

Break out of your narrow Mr. Right definition and expand your world to include men who are emotionally available and relationship ready, even if they don't "twinkle." Your love life and romantic future hang in the balance of this crucial choice.

- 16 -
I Want to Date a Man Just Like Me

NO

As a dating coach, I find more and more women want to date men with very specific criteria. Many women know exactly what they are looking for including energy level, activities and interests, and economic status or promise.

What about you? Do you know who you want to date? Take a moment right now to think about some personality qualities that you must see in a romantic partner. Is he charming, intelligent, affectionate, healthy, active, respectful, confident, independent and enjoys culture?

By coaching thousands of women, I have seen a common thread among the majority who do this exercise with me. These descriptions often actually describe a mirror image of the woman who is making the list!

Does that feel surprising to you? Think about it . . . would a man who is similar to your own personality really be a good match?

Whatever happened to opposites attract? What about someone with different interests who could broaden your life experience by sharing with you? What if the guy you are seeking is willing to do the activities you like sometimes if you join him in his favorites?

Let's get real about this. If you're looking for a reflection of yourself, you are going down a narrow path that sadly may go nowhere. Expecting a man to be just like you or like a girlfriend, is setting an incredibly unrealistic standard. It's a rare man who is going to exhibit these qualities, and if he does, will he have enough masculinity to satisfy your needs in a romantic partner?

I doubt it. The right man will likely never resemble you, or your girlfriends for one simple reason. HE IS NOT FEMALE. He is a MAN. Men are not like girlfriends (unless they are gay and then it's possible.)

Some similarities would be great of course. But, when you think about the couples you know — do you often see two introverts together or for that matter, two social butterflies? Not usually. One person is more reserved and the other is more outgoing. And that is just one example of the differences you might encounter. Some tension is required to feel the magic and the spark.

If you want a man to be "manly" about his life choices, his willingness to step up to the plate in a challenging situation, or to even take the lead so you can get a break — you'll need a masculine guy, not a surrogate girlfriend. Or you could end up with a man who has a lot of feminine energy, looking for a woman to take charge and take care of him. If that sounds right, there's nothing wrong with your choice. Just realize who and what you are choosing.

My point is — be in touch with the reality of who you are seeking as a partner. If this rings true for you, take time to re-think the personality you are seeking. What qualities do you feel you need? What will help you get along and seem compatible? What will make life fun and interesting? You may be surprised how you can acquire a taste for a few new characteristics that not only make it easier to find a man, but help you get along better and avoid previous pitfalls as well.

Lone wolf
Lone wolf
=
2 lone wolves

- 17 -

Perfection Won't Keep You
Warm at Night

After teaching a dating class one night, I ran into Barbara (who is single and 45) in the hallway. We exchanged surprised hellos and then she asked me what I was doing there. I replied, "I just taught a class called 'It's Never Too Late to Meet Mr. Right!'" Barbara rolled her eyes and exclaimed angrily, "There's no such thing as Mr. Right!"

At first I felt shocked because that's not the response I usually get. But, it was an honest, heartfelt comment. We took a couple of minutes to talk about what we each meant and then things started to become clear. Barbara's definition of Mr. Right is a man who is perfect, which explained why her reply was so emphatic.

Mr. Right Isn't Mr. Perfect

I don't mean to imply that when you find Mr. Right he'll be perfect. The truth is, nobody's perfect including you and me. The intent here is that you'll find the right man for you, not a perfect man. Someone who has a good mix of the qualities and an appreciation for the person you are, to create the magical bond that is love.

However, if you're like Barbara, searching for love with a vision of Mr. Perfect, as your dating coach I can only imagine the level of frustration you must be feeling. He has to be good looking, have a great sense of humor, be social, really smart, very successful, sensitive yet strong, emotionally available and stable, thoughtful, sexy, sweet, etc. Wow, that's a tall order!

Know What You Want in a Partner
As part of my dating coaching work with men and women, I recommend developing a list of the qualities you want in a partner. It's difficult to know if you have found the "one," if you don't know the qualities you're seeking. I also encourage culling the list down to the top five essentials, the characteristics you can't live without. Discernment is an important part of dating and this process offers a benchmark for your suitors.

However, the likelihood that you'll find a man with every single characteristic is slim. The top five are suggested to keep you realistic and focused on what's most important about your potential partner. You may find someone who has many of the qualities you desire, but expecting perfection is really a great way to stay single. If you find that you use your standards as rationale for rejecting every prospect, this could be evidence that you aren't as ready for a relationship as you think.

As you meet people, I hope you'll loosen up on perfection and consider more prospects. It's so easy to spend time judging each guy against every list item, but it's better to focus on how he does against your essentials. For example, can you simply connect, have a good conversation and some fun?

Ask yourself:

- ✧ Does he make me smile? ho did
- ✧ Is he a good person? yes

- ❖ Does he treat me well? _NO_
- ❖ Does he show me he's interested? _NO_
- ❖ Do I have fun when we are together? _yes 2x_

Your list isn't intended to be a stringent measuring stick, but rather, a guideline to ensure your basic needs are covered and to recognize what will make you happy. That's a very big difference. Look for a person's good points. The more you can appreciate the men you meet and see their positive traits, the more quality men you are likely to come across. Don't settle or lower your standards, but give men a chance by getting to know more of them.

Notice What Is Good
As you survey the room at the next singles' event, practice acknowledging what is good. Most people are naturally adept at seeing what isn't right. Noticing the positive will open your heart and mind to the abundance of great guys all around you. Let go of perfection and increase your chances for finding a good partner who will satisfy your top five list, add to your life, keep you warm at night, and make you happy over the long run.

This chapter is from my book *MANifesting Mr. Right: It's Never Too Late to Find the Love You Want*. Get your copy in paperback, as a downloadable ebook or as an MP3 audio file on CD at www.MANifestingMrRight.com

- 18 -
Are You a "Yes" Person or a "No" Person?

I saw a movie on TV with Jim Carrey called *The Yes Man*. As with many of his movies it was on the edge if not over. In the movie, Carrey takes a personal development workshop and commits to saying "Yes" to literally everything. His life takes a wild ride as a result, with many zany adventures.

When you think about it, saying "Yes" might actually have a tremendous impact for the better on your dating life. This is particularly true if you are prone to saying "No" which happens more frequently when dating after divorce or dating over 40. I ask my dating coaching clients, "What might you say "Yes" to?

- ✧ A blind date with a friend's brother.
- ✧ Posting a profile on Match.com.
- ✧ Meeting someone you connected with on a dating site
- ✧ Going to a singles dance with a friend or even solo.
- ✧ Trying speed dating.
- ✧ Talking to a good-looking stranger in a bar.
- ✧ Having a coffee date with a new man.
- ✧ Practicing your flirting skills.
- ✧ Finding the right man for you and falling in love.

73

That's a Powerful List with Loads of Possibilities
On the other hand, when you say "No", you limit
yourself drastically. Being discerning is appropriate
and smart. But limiting your opportunities
consistently minimizes the potential to achieve
your desires. This is true of both dating and life in
general.

When you say "No", you are literally keeping
yourself single. That's OK if you prefer your single
status. But if you want to find a loving partner,
saying "No" on a regular basis does not serve you.

Have You Ever Said "No" to Any of These Questions:

 - ✧ Can I have your number or email?
 - ✧ Would you like to meet me for a drink?
 - ✧ Would you like to dance?

I have. I'll never forget when I was 24, I was with
my friend Nancy and her boyfriend Scott playing
pool and this nice guy started talking to me and
joined our game. As we were leaving he asked for
my number. I didn't know what to do. Should I give
him the number or not? My friends said not to and I
felt torn. I left without divulging my digits.

To this day I wonder about him. We had similar
interests and he was easy to talk to. He seemed
like a nice guy and he was a carpenter, so he
could build and fix things. This was a crossroads in
my life. There was an ember ready to build into a
potentially nice fire, and I snuffed it out.

What about When You Say "No" to Yourself?
 - ✧ I hate those singles dances!

- ✧ I won't date a man who is bald.
- ✧ Men more than three years older than me are out.
- ✧ He's nice, but not my type.
- ✧ Blind dates just aren't my thing.

You could be missing opportunities that you'll never see when you say "No".

Saying "Yes", allows the Universe to help you meet your match. (This is another application of the Law of Attraction when like attracts like and saying "Yes" opens doors.) If you meet lots of men, the right man has a chance to cross your path. When you say "Yes" to situations and men, you are a pleasure to be with, living more fully and believe that all this effort will pay off.

And it will! It worked for me. It's worked for my dating coaching clients and for millions of women everywhere.

Just for Today, Catch Yourself When You Say "No"
Today, say "Yes" at least once when you want to say "No." You can become a "Yes" person and you can find the love you want. People find love every day. Say "Yes" and you could be next!

- 19 -
Men are People Too

You're out at a singles event hoping to meet Mr. Right. So, why does it feel like all the wrong men find you attractive? Where do the "good" men hang out? As a dating coach, I hear this question a lot. There are several answers and all of them could surprise you.

1) Is Your Guard Up or Do Men See You as Approachable?
When you go out, you usually hang with your girlfriends, facing each other toe-to-toe and talking up a storm. Did you know that you are sending nonverbal signals that you aren't open to anyone else approaching? Look at this from a man's perspective. Even if he thinks you're attractive, there isn't a way to easily break into your conversation.

As a woman, it's your job to make it easy for men! Talk with friends, but take time to look around the room, make eye contact and smile at people. Stand at an angle to each other, as if your bodies were forming the letter "V". This is the stance of two people open to a third to enter the conversation. That's one way to send the vibe that you're friendly and approachable.

2) Are You Willing to Talk to Men and Get to Know Them?
When a guy walks over to strike up a conversation, you usually shut him down immediately because he's not your type. He's too short, heavy, bald,

poorly dressed, unattractive, etc. While it's true, some things are incredibly obvious, people often make snap judgments that are dead wrong. How will you know? If you can just give a guy a chance by talking to him for a few minutes, you might discover he's interesting. Just because a man doesn't fit your perfect picture doesn't mean you should blindly send him packing.

3) Did You Know "Good Guys" Are Often Shy Guys?

Here's another reason that's even more important not to shut men down immediately: Good guys can often be shy guys who are watching how you interact with bolder, more confident men. If you turn away prospects abruptly, no shy guy will take the chance on you because he doesn't want to feel rejected. And that is your loss, not his. So think twice before you immediately reject a man because other men are watching how you treat people. As your dating coach, I hope you can see how significant this is.

4) Do You Believe "What Goes Around Comes Around?"

It's not that easy to walk across a room and speak to a stranger. Remember that men are people too. They have feelings, can be sensitive, and have fragile egos. Choosing to be kind, even if you aren't interested will serve you in the long run. That's because kindness often returns, although now always directly. This is part of the "What goes around comes around" philosophy of life and the Law of Attraction. Kindness attracts kindness, respect attracts respect.

The only obvious exception is if a man treats you poorly or threatens your safety. Then, do whatever is necessary to be smart and protect yourself.

5) Improve Your Attractiveness by Relaxing and Being Yourself
When you start thinking about men being people too, you take the pressure off meeting Mr. Perfect, let your guard down and start to enjoy getting to know them. This allows you to simply be yourself which demonstrates your confidence — a way to increase your attractiveness any time. The more men you talk to, the more comfortable you'll be — great practice for when you do encounter one of the "good guys."

Working with me as your dating coach, I'll encourage you to be friendly and treat men like regular people. You'll feel surprised at how quickly the positive feedback starts coming your way and your dating life improves.

- 20 -
Give the Good Guys a Chance

Women often grumble about the inventory of single men saying, "There are no good men available." Well new evidence is in and it's quite the contrary. I spoke with eight single men in their 40's who are members of a local dating service. What an eye opener! We spent an hour together discussing their surprising dating experiences. Hold onto your hats ladies because this is a shocker!

Who Are these Good Guys?
The group varied, but was very datable. Highlights included:

Career: teacher, electrician, IT consultant, insurance underwriter, mechanic.

Looks: 5'7" to over 6 feet; athletic to huggable; dark brown or salt and pepper hair to balding.

Education: two masters degrees to trade school.

Interests: cooking, biking, dancing, hiking, movies. Seems like a bunch of regular guys.

Men Want the Same Things You Want
Overall, the men expressed a sincere desire to find a loving relationship. Monogamy is a must and honesty is a primary concern. Most want a partner who is close in age (plus or minus five years.) Surprised? These men want exactly the same thing that most women want. So what's the

problem? Here's what the guys had to say about women and dating:

Women Won't Give Men a Chance
The men felt the biggest issue with women today is that the fairer sex just won't give them a chance. More often than not, the women they select from the dating service either say "No" without as much as a phone conversation or don't respond at all. As a result, the men feel bewildered, baffled, and very frustrated by this high level of rejection. They don't understand why women paid good money for a service they don't take full advantage of.

Men feel women's unwillingness to connect is because they are simply too picky and looking for a level of perfection that's unrealistic. The guys worry that they're too short, not fit enough, losing hair, don't have a status job, the right education, or make enough money. Hmmm, could they be right?

Working with me as your dating coach, we'll discover if this type of concern is holding you back from finding the love you want.

Look Past Looks
What fascinated me most is that the men complain about the very same thing that women complain about men! Women whine that men select or reject them based on looks alone rather than taking the time to get to know them. The truth is that selecting a potential partner based solely on physical attraction represents a trap that both sexes fall victim to. This is why most matchmakers don't use pictures with clients, insisting instead that they meet in person. Attraction is important to a good relationship, but is perfection necessary?

Missing the Boat on the Good Guys
All of this begs the question: What is the cost of turning men away based on superficial qualities? Seems like it might be pretty steep. Could be a lot of women are missing the boat on the "Good Guys" because they won't budge an inch to meet them. It's certainly something to think about. Of course, you must find a man attractive, but how important should looks be? Another good question is how much job status should be required for a man?

Expand Your Datable Criteria
When you think about the qualities you want in a partner, what comes first; fitness or a warm heart? A high-powered career or good communication skills? Education or honesty? In this day and age, when women feel fiercely independent and self-sufficient, do you really need his financial status or emotional support and friendship? Expanding your datable criteria opens the door for so many more possibilities.

Before you dismiss a man because of his physique, hairline, or job, try stretching yourself to discover what's good about him inside. Could he be worth a glass of wine, some light conversation, and 90 minutes of your time?

The bottom line on dating in the 21st century is this — Good men are available. If you're looking for a loving partner, ease up on stringent standards and let a few more prospects pass inspection. Give the next guy who approaches you a chance. Say "Yes" to a man who may not be ideal, but could be a wonderful partner just the same. You have little to lose, but the upside could be finding the love you've been seeking all along.

- 21 -
Open Your Heart to Love

Does your heart feel open to love and men? In case you could benefit from opening your heart a bit more, here's an easy and powerful visualization technique. Sit in a comfortable position and close your eyes. Become conscious of your breathing, slowly inhale and exhale to the count of seven, for at least three to five cycles. Imagine a beautiful pink rose or other multi-petal flower in bud form that resides in the center of your heart. The petals are fresh and tightly bound, protecting the delicate center. See the inherent beauty of this bud and all the fabulous potential it contains.

Next, give yourself permission to slowly and gently open that bud and your heart. In your mind, say these words, "I open my heart to love. May divine love flow through me, from me, and to me." Bathe yourself in this flow of love and feel it wash over you. Then, slowly, visualize the petals of your bud unfolding. Imagine them gracefully and tenderly unwinding, and loosening up bit by bit. The more the flower opens, the more your heart opens, and the more you feel the energy of love flowing all around.

Continue visualizing until the bud transforms into a fully blossomed flower, petals spread wide facing the sun. See it and yourself with all your amazing inner beauty. Lastly, express gratitude for this profound experience of love and your newly found openness. When you feel complete, open your eyes returning to full consciousness to enjoy a love-filled day!

This exercise can take as little as one minute or as long as 30 minutes. Choose the timing that feels right to you. If you notice any hesitancy in opening the blossom fully, feel free to stop where you are comfortable and then visualize a little more progress the next time you try the technique.

Practice this visualization if you have any concerns or negativity about men or love. If you want to find that genuine heart-connection with the right man, you'll need an open heart. The more you work with the exercise, the more you'll move through your day in an open manner. Men will see you as safe to approach and be more willing to start a conversation. Open your heart and watch what a difference it makes in your love life.

- 22 -

Are Your Actions Aligned with Your Intentions and Desires?

Elaine is 54, single, and an extremely busy executive with a job that is all consuming. Two weeks ago she went on a first date with Daniel, and she was complaining to me how he hadn't called. She felt surprised and confused to report that he had left a message just that day to set up their next date.

Elaine felt angry and apathetic about the second date. Two weeks was too long to wait and as a woman and a dating coach, I understand how she feels. But we didn't really have enough information to know for sure what had caused the time lapse. Maybe he doesn't have the same dating agenda. Maybe he's seeing several other women. Maybe he's not that interested. Maybe he was out of town on business. Regardless, it wasn't a good sign.

On the other hand, I pointed out that Daniel's pace was actually perfect for Elaine's busy schedule. Even if he had called sooner, Elaine was traveling on business and wouldn't have been able to get together. Plus, she isn't sure when she'll be able to set up the second date in the near future due to business and family obligations.

When you decide to work with me as your dating coach, we'll look below the surface to gain a deeper understanding of situations.

Elaine insisted she yearns for a loving, committed relationship. But, does she have time for it? Does she really want love? Reviewing her situation objectively, Elaine's actions do not match up with her desire. She doesn't have room for a man in her life and she does very little to find one or open up her time constraints. In other words, Elaine has not made finding love a priority.

We know this is true because after participating in dating coaching for months, she hasn't changed anything regarding her schedule or her efforts to meet men.

Hmm . . .

Let me draw an analogy. According to Feng Shui, when you have a bookcase jam-packed with books, that sends a message to the Universe that you are "all filled up" and don't need any more. That's the reason a Feng Shui practitioner will suggest you make room in that bookshelf and unload some of the titles. The same holds true for your TIME.

If you are like Elaine, busy, busy, busy and all booked up, you are sending a message to the Universe that you have everything you need. You have no more time, so why send anything else to you? Not the message you want to send is it?

To use the Law of Attraction properly, you not only have to focus on what you want, you have to take steps to find it as well. Elaine needs to align her actions with her desire and intention if she truly wants to find love.

I talked to Elaine about her time. How could she make room for some empty space — time that is left unplanned? That gave her a good chuckle. We talked about how she could read a couple of books that had been piled up if nothing came to fill the space. But she needed to start creating room in her calendar and her life if she wanted to send out vibes of being available. Elaine finally heard the message and saw how she was getting in her own way.

Deciding to work with me as your dating coach, I might ask you how you can make yourself more available. What can help is to clear the following areas of your life:

- ✧ Your mind
- ✧ Your heart
- ✧ Your closet
- ✧ Your calendar

These gestures help to free you up on multiple levels and make room for a man in your life.

If you feel any of Elaine's situation sounds like your life, you may want to start the clearing process too. Once you start to align your actions with your intentions, that is the surest way to attract what you want in life. Here's to clearing things up soon!

- 23 -
Self-Appreciation Increases Confidence for Dating

Ask any therapist and they will agree, all love starts with self love. This is very true since it is difficult to love anyone else without first loving yourself.

Here's a great way to build self-love. Make a list of your good qualities. What do you like about yourself? What are you proud of? For the purposes of this exercise, if you're a mom, do not resort to being a great mom. Self-love is all about you, not the people you care for.

Everyone has good points. Think about your physical aspects and your personality. Do you have a warm smile, slim legs, gorgeous hair, or great curves? As a person are you warm-hearted, laugh easily, smart, quick-witted, or philanthropic? Give yourself permission to write down everything that is good about you. Then read this list to yourself.

When you are done reading, close your eyes immediately. You want to feel the positive energy that emerges as you acknowledge yourself. Treasure everything that makes you unique and wonderful. Let your heart expand and fill with love and recognition for yourself. Connecting with self-love is an incredibly powerful method for opening your heart and life to new levels of loving energy.

Another powerful exercise is to look in the mirror and say to yourself, "I love you." This can be very confronting and many people cannot even complete the exercise, the discomfort is so great. Yet, you are the only one who knows you are doing this . . . so what's the problem?

People feel squeamish about self-love. However this is at the heart of finding a healthy, loving relationship. Repeat the exercise and with practice you will be able to look at yourself and admit you love yourself. It's not narcissistic — it's a very healthy step. Most people spend a good part of every day criticizing themselves and this exercise combats the countless negative messages you encounter from a variety of sources throughout the day.

Lastly, when you encounter rejection, (and if you're in the dating game, you will) look back to your list of what you love about yourself to lift your spirits and remind you why you are a great catch. Just because one person didn't recognize your "fabulosity" doesn't devalue all the wonderful qualities that make you special. As your dating coach, I recommend you look at that list daily to shore up your confidence and get back out there to find the love you want and deserve!

- 24 -

To Attract Love, Be Loving

Do you embody a loving attitude? According to the Law of Attraction made famous by "The Secret," like attracts like. By that logic, if you are working to attract love, you need to embody love and be loving. This might sound obvious to you, but see what you think of this example.

I was at a networking meeting last week where new members stood to introduce themselves. One woman I know said she had joined the group because she was new in town, wanted to meet people and make friends. After the meeting, she called me to say how disappointed she had been because not one person walked up to her to say "welcome" or introduce themselves.

At first I felt she was being ridiculous and her expectations seemed too high. But when I took time to think about it, I realized how right she was. So many people have become self-absorbed. Today, we are stretched to the max, trying to fit everything into a limited time frame. How can there be time for more? For new friends and experiences? To me, as a dating coach, my clients and others seem more isolated than ever, cocooning to spare themselves from an overly demanding world.

If you are someone with a loving attitude, you might at least introduce yourself and welcome someone new right? How else might you express your loving nature?

- ✧ Invite someone who is alone in a restaurant to join you for dinner.
- ✧ Check in with an elderly neighbor.
- ✧ Let people cut in front of you in line at the register or while driving.
- ✧ Donate your time to support a charity.
- ✧ Help a stranger in need.

As women, we tend to nurture, so I would expect many readers to say that they have listened to a friend or family member in need, brought food to someone ill, or baby sat in a pinch. That's great! But does your loving attitude shine through as you walk through the grocery store, cross a street or attend a singles dance?

Since you send nonverbal signals all the time, be sure you send out loving vibes. When you walk down the street, do your inner thoughts mostly criticize others or admire them? Do you judge people quickly or give them the benefit of the doubt?

To be your most attractive and approachable, you want to BE LOVING. I'll admit I am as guilty as the next person for being inwardly focused. But I challenge myself often to be aware of how I interact with others.

Embracing love as a way of moving through life, dramatically increase the opportunities to find love. Be loving as often as you can. Share your love with others. Show your appreciation for those who enrich your life. Reach out and lend a helping hand for those who express a need, and even those who don't.

Decide to work with me as your dating coach, and you'll become far more conscious of this loving energy and feel the surprising benefits. Let that loving energy radiate out from your heart and touch all those you come in contact with. Don't save it all for the perfect eligible bachelor — you won't get enough energy moving by waiting. Get your loving energy moving now and see what you attract as a result.

- 25 -

Love is a State-of-Mind

If you are in the process of looking for love, putting this important concept to work for you can make all the difference. Sometimes frustration can creep into your search which can cause your energy and attitude to plummet. As the Law of Attraction states "Like attracts like" which means it's a lot easier to find love if you feel and maintain a loving state-of-mind.

How can someone create a loving state-of-mind prior to finding the real thing? As your dating coach, let me share six powerful tips to help achieve a positive love outlook. You'll hear some ideas to improve self-love, while others enhance your attitude. See what appeals to you and put it to work to keep your spirits up and lovable.

1) Create a Sacred Space Dedicated to Love
Designate a sacred space and adorn it with a pair of pink candles, heart-shaped items, a framed picture of lovers from myth, movies or literature. You choose the symbols with the most meaning for you. Have fun with this task. When you look at your completed arrangement, it should instantly elicit warm, loving feelings and reinforce that finding love is really possible.

2) Heighten Your Feminine Charm
Wear perfume, sexy underwear or makeup to heighten your feminine charm. Put on your favorite outfit to feel fabulous. Get your nails done, have a facial or massage or try an aromatherapy session.

Take a bubble or scented bath, light the room with candles and play soothing or romantic music. Indulge in whatever makes you feel more alluring.

3) Focus on Your Best Features
Select your best feature and establish a daily practice to be grateful for its beauty. Every woman, without exception, has her own unique beauty and reason to be loved. Do you have beautiful eyes, sensuous lips, delicate hands, curvaceous hips or walk with a graceful step? Celebrate what makes you beautiful to build your self-esteem.

4) Practice Abundant Thinking
Notice the number of stars in the night sky or even cars on a traffic-jammed highway. Look for situations or items that are too numerous to count, because they provide excellent evidence that the Universe is an incredibly abundant place. When you feel abundant, you feel more generous and realize it's safe to share what you have, because there will always be more!

5) Think Loving Thoughts and Open Your Heart
Try smiling at someone who catches your eye, letting a person cut in front of you in the grocery store checkout, allow a car to leave a four-way stop ahead of you even if you were there first, etc. These random acts of kindness shift your energy and transform your life experience. This generosity of spirit might not be rewarded directly, but often comes back to you in other ways, even if it's just to maintain an elevated mood.

6) Find a Reason to Laugh at Least Once a Day
No matter what is happening in your life, there is always something to smile about. Some reasons

might include: feeling healthy, being employed, good weather, your favorite season, a happy memory, an upcoming vacation, friendship, family, a nice home, your pet, etc. Make a list of what is good and get in the habit of noticing what is going right with your world.

Don't feel you have to try all of these methods. But know that the more time you spend lifting your spirits and maintaining a positive self-image, the better your chances of feeling good and attracting the love your heart's desire. Choosing me as your dating coach, you'll start to feel this loving state-of-mind more often. At the very least, you'll enjoy whatever you do whole lot more. Knowing love is a state-of-mind makes it possible for everyone you encounter to experience it.

- 26 -
Open to New Ways of Meeting Men

It's not always easy to maintain a positive attitude and try new ways to meet people. Yet, feeling positive and having a willing spirit are crucial to your dating success. What can you do to encourage yourself to break from routine and experiment with new ways to meet people?

The Foundation for Out-of-the-Box Thinking
There is a key phrase that can be relied on as the foundation for out-of-the-box thinking and a positive outlook about looking for love: Try asking yourself "What the heck?" In other words, what's the downside of trying something new?

Free Yourself from Unfounded Fears
When asking my dating coaching clients what contributed to their dating success, so many respond, "I finally decided, 'What the heck?' and posted my profile, went to the dance, or said yes to the blind date." Saying "No" to these methods hadn't produced the results they wanted. Somehow these people managed to push past the fear and realize there was very little to lose except their single status.

They asked themselves, "What's the worst thing that could happen? What have I got to lose?" This is a great way to free yourself up from unfounded fears. The likelihood of meeting an axe murder is statistically quite slim.

Adopting a "What the Heck?" Attitude Moves You into Action

Trying anything new can cause trepidation for many people. But, without a willingness to explore various dating avenues, my happy clients who found love wouldn't be with their partners today. Adopting a "What the heck?" attitude helps you put aside fears in favor of action, to move toward the goal of meeting Mr. Right.

How Beth Met Sam

See what you think of this great example. Beth had been complaining she was having trouble meeting men, but admitted she was doing very little to change her luck. To shake things up, she thought "What the heck?" and posted her profile online, screened lots of responses and decided to meet a few of the men.

When Beth met Sam, she discovered they had a lot in common - in fact more than she realized because as it turns out, he lived right around the corner from her. Without posting her profile, Beth probably never would have met her neighbor Sam, who was an active, kind-hearted man with a great sense of humor.

Say "What the Heck?" to Limiting Thoughts Holding You Back

Sometimes people hold themselves back from meeting prospects because singles events seem daunting, or contrived. No problem! Take the pressure off and convince yourself that you have nothing to lose but those lonely weekends. Say "What the heck?" to limiting thoughts that keep you from trying new things and get on with finding the love you want!

- 27 -
9 Tips to Make
Finding Love a Priority

Is Your Love Life on the Back Burner?
Sometimes women allow their love life to sit on the back burner because they feel they don't have time. But, could it be they don't make the time? How realistic is it to expect the dream of a loving relationship to come true, without making any effort?

As mentioned earlier in chapter one, there is a principle in Hawaiian Shamanism that states, "Energy flows where attention goes." In other words, what you choose to focus on is where your energy automatically goes. Where do you want to put your energy? You can long to meet someone OR you can do something about it. Consciously choosing love as a priority is what makes it possible.

Finding Love Is Like Any Other Goal
To achieve any goal, action steps have to get on your "to do" list. This is why finding a mate is no different than any other objective, like getting into shape, saving for retirement and finding a new job. For any of these achievements to materialize, you need to concentrate on it, create an action plan, and commit to executing it.

The Best Time to Get Started
It's easy to busy yourself with the daily grind, and avoid meeting new people. Doing something new can feel uncomfortable and procrastinating is part

of human nature. So, how can you make finding love a priority? Ask yourself this question, "If not now, when?" You can start tomorrow, in two weeks or two years. The choice is yours. But, as your dating coach, I ask you—how will putting it off help you meet someone? If you truly desire a loving relationship, NOW is the best time to take the first step.

Fear is a natural emotion that often accompanies any new endeavor. You may feel uncertain of where to start or what to do first. Keep in mind this simple Chinese proverb, "The journey of a thousand miles begins with a single step." Even a small step counts, like mentioning to a few friends that you would like to meet someone.

Suggestions to Get Started
Here is a list of ideas that will get you started on the road to finding love. Allow yourself to feel excited about a couple of options and you see how easy it is to start meeting new people.

1. Look in the newspaper for a calendar listing of singles events and pencil a few on your own calendar.

2. Attend a live speed dating event — visit one of these sites to learn more: 8minutedating. com, Hurrydate.com, Speeddating.com.

3. Find out if your Church or Synagogue holds singles events or dances and go!

4. Enlist a friend as your dating buddy and motivate each other to get out there.

5. Sign up for online dating, get some good photos, create an interesting profile and get started.

6. Check sites like Singlesonthego.com or CraigsList.org.

7. Mention to your friends, family, neighbors, and associates that you feel ready to meet someone to share life with. This is the best way to generate blind dates!

8. Hire a matchmaker to do the search for you! You probably have a financial planner or an accountant, so why not work with a dating professional to find the love you want?

9. Decide to hire me as your dating coach to motivate, inspire, and provide you with the keys to effective dating today.

The Only Thing You Have to Lose is Your Single Life

You have nothing to lose and everything to gain by getting your dating campaign underway. Why wait? There are plenty of good people who would be thrilled to have your love and support. The only way you are likely to meet the "one," is to get out there.

Make finding love a priority in your life. Don't wait another day to connect with the love you deserve. You may feel a bit uncomfortable at first, but nothing ventured, nothing gained! And what you feel when you find love makes everything you did to completely worthwhile.

- 28 -
Wrapping It All Up

This book has covered so many negative thought processes that can easily keep you single and from the love you want. You've read and learned how to:

- ✧ Find plenty of good men if you are willing to be friendly, talk to them and give them a shot.
- ✧ Open your heart and love yourself.
- ✧ Stay focused and not be derailed by unrealistic expectations that keep you cut off from possibilities.
- ✧ Push past normal fears and get out of your comfort zone to try something new.

As your dating coach, I have shared some of my best tips, insights and exercises to improve your dating process and ensure your success. Let me show you how good it feels to align your desires with your intentions as you see and hear how to manifest the love life you long for.

Having worked with thousands of women, what I know is this:

Finding love is real
Finding love is possible
Finding love is your destiny!

Take the steps now to get started. Use these methods to transform your toxic thoughts that keeps you from love. Open your eyes, mind and heart to see that love can be yours. Get out there to cross paths with the right man for you.

I found love after giving up all hope. I managed to transform my negative and misguided thinking to turn things around and get married to a wonderful man. The right man for me. I know deep in my heart you can do it too!

Biography

Ronnie Ann Ryan, MBA, CCC, is an internationally-known Dating Coach, professional speaker, workshop leader and author of *MANifesting Mr. Right* who has helped thousands of single women transform their love lives and to find the amazing man they dream of. Ronnie has appeared at Long Wharf Theatre, and has been interviewed by BBC 5Live Radio, FOX and ABC News, Sally Jesse Raphael, NPR, WYBC with Lisa Wexler, WPLR, WELI, Star99, MSN.com, and MORE.com, plus a variety of other print, broadcast and web articles in the US, UK and Australia.

Contact Information:
www.MANifestingMrRight.com
www.NeverTooLate.biz
Blog: www.after40datingtips.com
Ronnie@NeverTooLate.biz
203-877-3777